MW01656952

TW[O] CITIES THAT BURNED

Genesis 18:16—19:30
FOR CHILDREN

Written by Lucille B. Golphenee
Illustrated by Gordon Willman

ARCH Books

Copyright © 1983 CONCORDIA PUBLISHING HOUSE,
3558 SOUTH JEFFERSON AVENUE,
ST. LOUIS, MISSOURI
MANUFACTURED IN THE UNITED STATES OF AMERICA
ISBN 0-570-06168-7

Oh, Sodom and Gomorrah, we read,
Were two cities long ago.
The people there were very bad;
The Bible tells us so.

It made the Lord so very angry
When He saw the things they'd done.
He said, "I'll send down a rain of fire
And destroy them, every one."

He sent three angels forth to see
His servant Abraham,
Who fixed some food for them, and then
They told him of God's plan.

This good man had a nephew, Lot,
Who lived in Sodom too,
And Abraham was worried when
He heard what God would do.

And so he pleaded with the Lord
To save his kinfolks' life:
"Oh please, God, spare my nephew Lot,
His daughters, and his wife!"

The Lord was ever gracious,
And He sent, from heaven above,
His angels to protect them
In His mercy and His love.

To lead them out and bring them in
To a place of sweet safety,
So when the time of trouble came,
Secure they all would be.

Then Lot received them gladly,
Brought them in to spend the night.
He baked some bread and fixed a meal
And treated them just right.

The wicked people of that place
Then gathered 'round about.
They said to Lot, "We saw these men;
Come on and bring them out."

Then Lot was very, very sad,
Because he knew that they
Would try to hurt these friends of his.
He said, "Please go away!"

The men grew angrier with him
And said, "We'll kill you too."
Then Lot was very much afraid
And did not know what to do.

He tried to reason with them,
But they would not even hear;
So Lot went back into the house,
As they all gathered near.

And so the angels struck them blind,
And they could see no more.
They staggerd here and there all night,
But could not find the door.

So then the angels said to Lot,
"Take all your family dear
And get out of this wicked place.
Now hurry! Do you hear?

"We're going to burn this city up;
The people are so bad.
If you don't get right out of here,
You'll surely wish you had."

Lot went to see his sons-in-law
And told them of God's plan,
But they just laughed at him and said,
"Go on, you silly man."

Then, as Lot waited yet a while,
The angels took his hand
And said, "Now it is time to go
And leave this wicked land.

"For we cannot do anything
Until you all are gone.
The fire of God is going to fall,
And it will not be long."

Lot's wife and daughters went with him.
The angels led them out,
And said to run and not look back
To see what came about.

As soon as they were gone from there,
The fire from heaven did fall—
Burned up those wicked people
And destroyed them, one and all.

The angels said to not look back,
But Lot's wife disobeyed.
She turned and took a longing look,
And with her life she paid.

She turned into a lump of salt
Because she did not mind;
And so her family all escaped,
But she was left behind.

So Lot came into Zoar,
For his girls a home to make.
The angels told him they would spare
That city for his sake.

But they did not live there for long,
Since Lot was scared to stay.
They made a home inside a cave,
And stayed there night and day.

They were so happy to be safe
And find a lodging there,
They kneeled and prayed with grateful hearts
And thanked God for His care.

Dear Parents,

Rather than focusing on the fate of the two cities, the story concentrates on the efforts to rescue believing Lot and his family. Abraham pleaded with God to spare Sodom. (What an example for us!) Then the angels, God's messengers, again and again had to urge Lot and his family to leave the city. They seemed to resist God at every step, when He was trying to save them.

How much like us! We, too, so often resist God's gracious efforts to help us. But still He persists. And finally He leads us to a place of safety.

Help your child to see that God can keep us, His dear children, safe "in the midst of a crooked and perverse generation among whom [we] shine as lights" (Philippians 2:15). We who believe in Jesus Christ and His atoning work are of special concern to our heavenly Father. He will not let us perish.

The Editor